Come
LET ME TELL YOU

First paperback edition May 2023

Book design by Leighton Williams
Illustration by Calvin Morgan

ISBN: 9798392375714

Published by Paths and Gateways

Come LET ME TELL YOU

Come let me tell you is a collection of short stories written by children attending primary (elementary) schools in rural Jamaica.

Each story and title are original work from these children. The stories will captivate you, reminding you of the innocence, emotions, experiences, and imagination we had when we were young.

Please enjoy these great stories, read aloud with friends.

Illustrations by
Calvin Morgan

Appreciation

Stephanie Outten

Leighton Williams

Jodi-Ann Davis Walker

Desrene Williams Taylor

Taffari Sewell

Latoya Samuels
Principal, WhiteHill Primary and Infant

Crystal Daye

Shyan Robinson
Carisbrook Primary and Infant

Yanique Brown
Merrywood Primary

Calvin Morgan

Recognition

All students who participated in the Paths and Gateways
Storywriting Competition.

Table of Content

My Favourite Christmas Holiday

by
Mickaylia Wallace

It was a beautiful Saturday afternoon in December 2022. While having my lovely bowl of chicken foot soup, the phone rang. It was my aunt Angella from St. Catherine asking if I would like to come and spend the Christmas holiday with her. I was so excited I jumped with joy. This would be my first time leaving home since the Covid-19 pandemic. I ran to my room and started packing all my clothes. A little while after my mom, my mom came into my room and said "guess what! your aunt said your friends whom you had met the last time you were by her house are inviting you to their Christmas party." The feelings I had were unexplainable, my suitcase was packed within minutes.

The following day my aunt came to pick me up in her Sports Utility Vehicle (SUV) and my holiday began. I sat in the front of the car beside my aunt with my seatbelt on and waved goodbye to my mom and grandmother. The drive from the country was an experience to be remembered. I travelled through three different parishes in one day. We went from St. Elizabeth to Manchester, then to Clarendon and finally reached St. Catherine to my aunt's house. When I got to the house I was so tired. Luckily, we ate while travelling so I just crawled into bed and went straight to sleep.

A few days later, it was time for the Christmas party. The decorations were something to talk about. I couldn't wait for the party to be over to collect some of the beautiful balloons. At the party we exchanged gifts, and I received a beautiful long-haired doll. I had so much fun, it was a party to remember.

After leaving the party we went to the Community Treat they

had for us children. They had a Ferris wheel, a bounce-a-bout and a trampoline. Not only that, but my aunt and I went to the grand-market event in the town. Oh, it was a blast! I was having so much fun; the excitement of seeing all the fireworks blasting into the sky. It was magnificent! There was a huge Christmas tree in Rose Duncan's Park filled with pepper lights and beautiful decorations.

A lot of people were taking pictures, a man was spinning a machine which made cotton candy and I had so much food to eat. I ate KFC, popcorn, and peanuts, just to name a few. We didn't reach home until Christmas morning and then I realized I had an upset stomach from eating so many different things. My aunt had to give me a cup of Ginger tea, and I asked her if I could go ahead and open my Christmas presents from under the tree before I went to sleep. We all unwrapped our presents at the same time and I got a beautiful kitchen and a doll set. After that, I went to bed.

I woke up by mid-afternoon, to see my aunt and cousin cooking. They were as my mother would say 'cooking up a storm' of rice and peas, fried chicken and fish, and roasted beef. I offered to help by shredding the vegetables. I really enjoyed my Christmas dinner and after we had fruitcake and ice cream.

After all that eating, I went and had my bath and put my Christmas dress on. My aunt said, "let's go for an evening walk" and she took some of our delicious dinners to her neighbour's house.

This was my favourite Christmas holiday ever.

The Day I Made Someone Smile

by
Trodrae Cowan

It was Monday, January 23, 2023. I got off from school at 2:30pm. I remember passing an old couple on the side of the road begging for food. I decided at that time, I wanted to put a smile on their faces. I went to the bank and withdrew ten thousand dollars and went in search of the elderly couple. As I was walking along the road, I noticed a tall, angry-looking man of dark complexion wearing all black briskly walking behind me. I became very concerned, so I took a detour onto another road. To my surprise he was still following me, so I switched to another street. The man was very determined and continued to follow me.

I was now in a panic wondering how I was going to escape this stranger. Suddenly, here comes the same old couple out of nowhere. They started annoying the man, begging him for food. He was so distracted; I hid in the nearby shop and watched him bully the couple because they interrupted his plan. Feeling defeated, he angrily left in the opposite direction. I stayed hidden for a while to ensure that the coast was clear. I then went and found the elderly couple and thanked them for saving me. I explained to them that I was searching for them to give them the money I withdrew to buy the food they needed. They were very grateful, and I felt great putting a smile on their faces.

The Scariest Day of My Life

by
Danae Brown

One day, I went to my grandma's house. Everyone went shopping except my sister, my grandma and myself. My grandma went to sleep while my sister watched TV. I felt like feeding aunt Sash's chickens in the backyard so I went for a bowl of rice. I left the door open and went into the backyard with the chickens. Suddenly, the door went BANG! I started to wonder what was happening because there was no wind. I ran and opened the door and I saw a black figure running through the hallways and it turned into my room. It had long hair and was dressed in all white. I ran after it to my room, but when I got there it was gone. I told my sister, but she did not believe me.

Thirty minutes later, we heard a loud CRUNCH! In the kitchen. When we went to check the sound, we screamed AHHHHHHHH!!!. There was nothing there but a bag of chips. Grandma came in at the same time and said she heard a knock on the door. It was not Halloween so no one should be knocking on the door. I was so scared. My mother, Kerry, called a few minutes later. I told her what was happening, however, she said she was going on a business trip and I could not come along. I was devastated. Then I felt like something touched me. I was trying to call out to my grandmother but there was no sound coming out of my mouth. I tried to get off the bed, but I could not move.

Then suddenly there was a dark shadow over my bed. I kicked and screamed for help, but I was overpowered by the shadow. I remembered that my grandmother told me about something similar that happened to her when she first moved into her new home. I started shouting and kicking and screaming even harder.

Then I felt a cold hand shaking my foot. I jumped up panicked. Only to find out it was all a dream.

The Beautiful Horse

by
Kayanna Hinds

The day started with beautiful sunshine adorning the flowers and the trees in the field. Mr Joe woke up and stared into the beautiful sky and smelled the fresh grass waving good morning in the breeze. His grandson came running, "good morning grandpa! How are you? I would like some of your hot chocolate tea this morning." Mr Joe replied, "yes mi grandboy, you can have some." His grandson took the hot chocolate tea and drank it. "Mmmm! I love the taste of hot chocolate!" then they set off to work.

Mr Joe and his grandson cleared and ploughed the farmland and then planted some carrot seeds. They worked until they saw a black horse standing in the distance. They paused and wondered to themselves why the horse was standing there. They have never seen a horse so beautiful. They continued to work until they were tired. Mr Joe decided that it was time for them to go to lunch because he was hungry. "What did you bring for lunch grandpa?" asked Mr Joe's grandson. "Well me grandboy, me bring some ackee and saltfish and fry dumpling me cook dis morning. Plus, me have little lemonade," replied Mr Joe. They ate until their bellies were full.

Mr Joe continued to clear another field after lunch. The horse they saw in the distance began to gallop and they started to chase it. They ran until the horse was far away in the distance. Mr Joe's grandson said he was tired and wanted to go home. Grandpa agreed it was time to go. While on their way home, they saw the horse again and this time it started to follow them. They saw a lady who told them how beautiful the horse looked. Mr Joe explained that the horse was not theirs but it just started following them home.

His grandson told the lady that he hopes when the horse comes home with them, they can keep him because he is so beautiful.

The Story of King Ashton

by
Jayden Tennant

Ashton lived for many years and was famous. He was always busy doing what was necessary to provide food for his family. One day, Ashton and his warriors were together, going out to find water for cooking at a big parade event. I wanted to go with them, so I shouted "stop!" But it was too late, he was on a donkey heading towards his palace. Suddenly he glanced behind him and saw me. He stopped and said, "I know you. Come with me." I was so shocked I went with him. Upon arrival at his palace, I realized how huge and busy it was. King Ashton invited me inside to have dinner with him. I was overwhelmed and stacked with excitement, so I accepted his invitation. Why would I refuse?

As I sat at the huge shiny gold table looking at the buffet I got more excited. There were all types of foods, curried chicken, baked chicken; orange, apple, mango, tamarind juice, and so much more. After the waiters served me my food, the king and I started talking about crops. I soon noticed some of the warriors fighting and one attacked the king. I looked to my left and saw a knife and quickly stabbed the warrior who attacked the king. I was so scared because I thought the king would punish me for killing his warrior, but to my surprise, he thanked me with teary eyes, "thank you for protecting me. Thank you. Thank you!" He then fell in love with me, came up to me and put a ring on my finger at that moment for my loyalty. King Ashton looked deep into my blue eyes while I stared into his deep brown, bright, shiny eyes and he whispered, "you are my queen and my lover. I will put you in my palace.

Danielle, know what you mean to me because of what you did

today." He continued, "You are my neighbour and you defended me, so I want to surprise you. But first I need to tell you something." King Ashton gulped and breathed a sigh of relief. He told me that when he was five, his father left him and his mom. His mother blamed him for it, and he was so mad that his father left but that only made his mother angrier at him. His father came back when he was nine years old but disappeared three months later without a trace. This made his mother even angrier and she blamed him again. His mother died before he could make her happy and so he promised to make me happy. I felt sorry for King Ashton, so I hugged him and then we headed out for an evening party.

George's Sad Life

by
Adrian Jones

There was a nineteen-year-old boy named George who lived with his father Kevin and his older sister Sophie, in a poor immigrant neighbourhood of New York City. George's father is a silent man who worked nights in a fish market and Sophie worked in a cafeteria in The Bronx. Their mother died in a terrible car accident when George was five and Sophie was thirteen years old. The family lives in a railroad flat, one in which each leads to the next, in a straight line like the cars of a railroad train. George's life was not easy. He has dropped out of school and has no job or friends. With no mother, an uncommunicative father and a sister away at work all day, George is lonely. He lacks companionship, love, and guidance. In his community, George feels a sense of alienation and feels no connection to those around him.

One day, George decided to go and seek a job from Mr Bailey. Mr Bailey owned a supermarket in the town. He asked Mr Bailey to hire him, but he said no because George had no experience. George was extremely disappointed, but he did not give up his search for a job. He decided to go to Mr Robert, who owned a car mart, to see if he could get a job there without any experience. On his way to Mr Robert's car mart, someone told George his father was in the hospital after suffering from a heart attack. George rushed as fast as he could to the hospital. When George got to the hospital, he saw his sister sitting and crying. George sat down beside her and asked how their father was doing.

Sophie said their dad was in critical condition and George broke down and started to cry. Two months passed and then their father passed away. Sophie and George were devastated and heartbroken. Two years later, they became successful business owners.

My Trip To The Cayman Islands

by
Keith-Ray White

One night I heard my mom talking to my father on the phone about a trip to the Cayman Islands. Mom told dad that she wants to travel there with me. My father agreed and said he would pay for the tickets so we could come and see him. My father bought overnight tickets for us and on December 2, 2019, we went to the airport in Kingston. We checked in at the front desk and security checked our bags and hand luggage so we could board the plane. We travelled with the Cayman Airway airline.

I went and sat at the seat with the number I was given; my seat was close to the window. I could see everything that was taking place outside the window. As we took off, I saw the beautiful sea, and the roads with vehicles, houses and other aeroplanes. Everything looked so small from in the air. As we went higher into the sky, we went into patches of clouds and the plane felt shaky for a while before returning to normal. I had to pee so I went to the bathroom and on my way, I felt the plane turn right. When I came back I felt dizzy. Thirty minutes later the plane landed in Cayman.

We came off the plane and went inside the airport where I saw my father standing, waiting for me. I ran as fast as I could with my suitcase to hug him. When we left the airport, I looked to my left and I was shocked to see that the airport runway was so close to the main road. I must say that the Cayman Islands is ninety percent similar to Jamaica because a few of the houses were made out of wood and the others out of blocks. My father got us a taxi so we could all go to his rented house. When we got there, I noticed that the house was very small.

After unpacking, my dad said he was going to cook chicken foot soup for our dinner. He cooked the soup and we all had dinner before taking a bath. When we were finished he told my mom and I that he would take us to the supermarket in the morning. The next morning we went to the supermarket and bought chicken, carrots, pork and rice. We cashed out our groceries and headed home. In the evening we went to watch other planes take off and land and my dad took me to a playground. I played for an hour and then went home. At home, we watched a movie named 'Top Gun Maverick' until I fell asleep.

The next morning, mom and dad woke me up to go to the beach in George Town. We went to Key Bay Beach and the first thing I saw was a lot of people and sand castles. Dad walked my mom and I around the beach for a while. We stopped and drank coconut water and made some new friends. We enjoyed the beach and afterwards, we went home and had chicken for dinner. I took a bath and went to bed because I was really tired. A few days later, mom said it was time to come back to Jamaica. I was really sad but visiting the Cayman Islands was the best experience of my life.

The Scariest Movie I watched

by
Shannel Harding

One day, my friends and I were watching a scary movie named 'IT'. The first thing that happened in the movie was that a boy named Bill helped his little brother Georgie to make a paper sailboat. Georgie wanted to go outside and sail the boat in the heavy rain but Bill was too tired to join him. The brothers hugged before Georgie ran out to play. Georgie sailed his boat down the street and chased after it. The paper sailboat accidentally ran into a roadblock and sailed to the end of the street and into a sewage drain. Georgie ran and tried to catch it before it disappeared.

As he looked into the drain, Georgie saw a pair of yellow eyes; it was a clown named Pennywise. The boy talked with the clown for a while and asked for his help to get his boat. However, the clown refused to help him get the boat and instead, he held Georgie's hand and bit it off with his big teeth. The little boy tried to get away from the drain but the clown ate him. I was so shocked at this that I paused the movie. I wanted to stop watching it but I was so interested in seeing what happened next so I continued to watch.

Then, a little girl popped up on the screen. It was so frightening I held my chest. The girl went to use the bathroom but when she looked into the sink she realized it was blocked. She could not tell what blocked it, so she went for her dad's tape measure and measured the hole. Suddenly, something held her face and blood came out of the sink and splattered everywhere. Hearing the loud noise in the bathroom her dad came to see what the problem was but he could not see the blood. The next day her friends visited her house to see if they were able to see the blood.

When they went to the bathroom, they saw that the blood was everywhere and helped her to clean it, then they went home.

Two days later, a boy named Taylor was in the library reading a book when he saw a red balloon. Taylor followed the red balloon and then he saw someone coming down the stairs, but he did not have a head. He began to chase Taylor and Taylor ran away and bounced into the librarian. Taylor never went back to the library building again. After I watched that scary movie, I became really afraid at home. I am scared of going into the kitchen and the bathroom mostly because of what I watched. Now, I take my little brother everywhere around the house with me to keep me company.

My First Pet Goldfish

by
Odjhauni Harding

It was a bright and sunny morning and my mom and I were preparing to go to the carnival in the city of San Juan. I was excited to go because I had never been to the carnival. "Mom, can I have a pet goldfish please," I asked. "No!" she replied, "pets are a big responsibility and I don't think you are old enough to take care of a pet. I was very disappointed. Although I was really sad, I hurriedly got dressed and got in the car and we drove to the carnival. When we arrived mom asked me what I wanted to eat and I shouted ice cream. I got my favourite flavour, eggnog, and it was delicious.

Then I asked my mom to go and ride the Ferris wheel and she said yes. I waited about five minutes then it was my turn. I stepped up onto the ladder and sat in my seat so the operator could buckle me in. I screamed with excitement as the ride went higher and higher as it spun around. The ride came to an end and a kind gentleman unbuckled me from the seat. Then it was time for my favourite part of the carnival, the pet shop. I saw a lot of different animals, but my eyes were fixed on the aquariums with the goldfish in them. A man was shouting, "$100 for a throw. If you hit the red dot you can have whatever pet you want."

I was excited to try and win my very first pet goldfish. In a low voice, I asked my mom if I could try, and she gave in and said yes. I stood in the long line and waited for my turn. I really wanted the goldfish, so I aimed and tossed the dart gently at the spot with my eyes closed. "We have a winner!" shouted the man. When I opened my eyes he was holding a bowl with a goldfish in it. I was so excited, I turned to the fish and said,

"I will name you Pebbles." I was in such a hurry to take her home that I forgot I needed to stop at the store to get her an aquarium. My mom quickly reminded me, and we went to the pet store.

We bought Pebbles an aquarium and fish feed for her. I told mom not to worry because I will feed her and ensure that her aquarium is cleaned at least twice per week.

My First Time In America

by
Javari Duncan

A few years ago, I went to America for the very first time. I was so excited when I heard my mom say that she was going, I asked if I could go too and she said yes. I was so excited I packed my clothes the same day, December 30, 2017, even though the trip was not until January 4, 2018. Every day I prayed for January 4 to be tomorrow until January 4 finally came. I was so happy, I quickly took a shower and got dressed while the car waited for us at the front of the house. I rushed into the car, while my mom and the driver packed the suitcases in the car.

On our way to the airport, we stopped in Middle Quarters to buy shrimp to eat from the street side vendors. We did not stop again until we reached the airport in Montego Bay. We took some photos before we went inside to check-in. We waited for about an hour before we were able to board the plane. We were told to sit and put our seatbelts on so the plane could take off. The plane became very noisy and started shaking and moving fast. It took off from the runway and when I looked down from my window seat, I saw cars, buildings, roads and the deep blue sea.

Two hours later, we landed at the Orlando airport in Florida. My mom collected our suitcases and we checked out and went outside. I was so excited when I saw my sister and uncle that I ran and hugged them tightly. When we were driving to my sister's house I saw a lot of cars and tall buildings with pretty lights. On our way, we ordered Chick-fil-A for dinner and when we got home I went straight to bed. In the morning, my sister made us breakfast and I ate and took a shower because I was going to the mall with my mom and uncle.

When we got to the mall, I was so shocked and excited to see lots of kids' rides, ice cream shops, popcorn machines and different game shops. I asked my mom to play on the rides and she said yes. I had a lot of fun then my uncle took me to the Polo store and bought me lots of clothes and slippers. Then it was time to go back to my sister's house. I spent the rest of my time in America, visiting stores like Walmart and Ross and eating a lot of junk food like KFC and Mcdonald's. America is such a big and beautiful place. I had a great time, especially when I went to the waterpark and the huge game centre.

After a few weeks, my mom said it was time to come back to Jamaica. I was really sad that I had to leave but my mom promised that we would visit America again.

Sam and Tom With the Lost Dog, Max

by
Rovantay Knight

One day Sam and Tom were playing together in the yard. They saw a dog that seems lost, so Sam went over to the dog and decided to take him in. He looked so hungry and tired that they could not have left him there. They took him to the kitchen and fed him Dog food and milk. It was getting late but no one asked for the dog or reported him missing. When their parents got home and saw the dog, they asked Sam where it came from. He told him he found it wandering outside while we were playing in the yard. Their parents told them that if no one came for the dog and they wanted to keep him, they would have to be responsible because dogs needed to be cared for.

A few days later, the boys named the dog Max since no one claimed him and he had no collar. It was about 6 am when the boys got up one morning to the loud barks of the dog. They rushed outside to see what happened to Max, but to their surprise, he was wagging his tail and jumping in excitement to see them. The boys pet the dog and went inside to get ready for school. When they got to school, they told all their friends about the new dog and invited them to come over and help them build a dog house. Their friends were excited and after school, they grabbed all the necessary tools and went to Sam and Tom's house to build a doghouse for Max. They bought Max a bowl and a mat so he would have a place to eat and sleep. It was a very long day for them, playing with Max and building his house, so Sam and Tom decided to bathe Max before his dinner. For dinner, Max got rice and sardines and water. He quickly ate it and then curled up on his mat and fell asleep. The next morning, Sam and Tom took

Max for a walk in the park. At the park, they played fetch with a red ball which is Max's favourite and he loved it.

The Out Speaker

by
Shalmell Morgan

One beautiful and sunny Saturday in December, Melissa was woken up by the sun in her eyes coming from her room window. She woke up, yawned lazily, and turned her back to the window. Just then a family member barged into her room with a big birthday cake and party hats exclaiming, "HAPPY BIRTHDAY MELISSA!" She jumped out of bed in amazement wondering how she could have forgotten her twelfth birthday. She quickly blew out the candles on the cake and told her family members to meet her downstairs while she does her casual morning routine. She took a shower, brushed her teeth, combed her hair, and got dressed.

When she went downstairs it seemed as if the tables were also telling her a happy birthday. Her mother had already started sharing the cake among the household members. Just then Melissa gasped realizing that she would be starting school. She told her mother she was really scared of going to school because of her condition. Her older brother Mark laughed at her and said, "You have all right to be scared, you look like a freak!" Melissa felt embarrassed and burst into tears and ran to her room. Mr Wilson sent Mark to his room while their mother went to comfort, Melissa. Her mother told her beauty is on the inside and that if someone truly loves her, they will love her despite her condition. Melissa stopped crying immediately and continued to enjoy her weekend. Soon, it was Monday morning. Melissa woke up and did her casual routine. By the time she finished, it was around 6:30 am and she rushed downstairs just in time to see her mother preparing breakfast. "Good morning mom," said Melissa. "Good morning honey how was your night?" responded mom. "It was okay,"

answered Melissa. Mrs Wilson smiled. A few minutes later Mark and Mr Wilson came downstairs, and they all had breakfast together. After breakfast, Mrs Wilson packed their lunches while Mark warned Melissa not to let anyone know they are related because he is very popular and dating the principal's daughter. He told her it would be bad if everyone found out he was related to someone with dermatographia. Before she could react their father came and told them to get into the car for school.

They waved goodbye to their mother and Mr Wilson kissed her on her forehead. Twenty minutes later they arrived at school. Melissa remembered Mark's warning and went in the opposite direction. She then met a girl named Samantha Morgan who offered to be her friend and showed her around the campus. At lunch, Melissa went into the bathroom and saw a group of girls bullying a girl. Melissa tried to make them stop but they just continued. Samantha ran into the bathroom and Melissa told her what was going on and they both reported it to the principal. In the cafeteria, the girls started bullying Samantha and Melissa for getting them in trouble. Mark also joined in the bullying and told everyone about her illness. Melissa ran from the cafeteria and into the school's garden. In the garden, she accidentally bumped into a tall boy around the same age as her, who questioned why she was running in the garden. Melissa told him she was hiding from Monica and the other girls that bullied her. As it turns out the boy was Samantha's brother, Mike, and he was also hiding in the garden because he was bullied about his mismatched eyes. When Melissa got home, she ran straight for her room and burst into tears thinking about her day. Realizing what he had done Mark confessed to his father and was grounded. Melissa decided to start writing music to make her feel better and started publishing songs that went viral.

Even though Melissa was popular because of her songs she was still bullied at school during lunch and cried every evening when she came home. Mike and Samantha would always visit her and the people in her community would encourage her to continue writing music and ask for her autograph. One day during lunch, her brother and his girlfriend came to bully her because of her condition and she recalled the wise words of her mother, "beauty is not on the outside but on the inside". Monica and Mark were speechless by Melissa's response and everyone in school applauded her for standing up to them. Eventually, Melissa graduated from High School, at the top of her class and in her Valedictorian speech forgave her brother and Monica.

A few years later, Melissa became a police officer and started dating Mike. She and Samantha were still best friends and told each other everything. Monica and Mark continued dating for a while but ended when Monica's dad left her and her mom homeless and poor on the side of the street. Melissa, with the help of Mike and Samantha, started a charity for homeless people to help Monica and her mom off the street. Mike and Melissa got married and had a beautiful baby named Daniel. Melissa hired Monica as her babysitter and opened a Primary School called 'Carisbrook Primary and Infant School'. Daniel grew up in a loving household that taught him not to bully anyone because their conditions are unique and they all lived happily ever after.

My Summer Holiday

by
Samora Waite

It was the last day of school, and everyone was excited about summer. You could hear all the students talking about what they were going to do for the holiday. I was telling my friend John that I'm going on a trip to a hotel located beside a beach but the bell rang and we all went home. The next day my mother, father, brother and sister and I all got ready to go to the hotel. After a long drive, we arrived at the hotel and instantly changed and went to the beach. The sky was clear, the wind was cool and everyone was having fun. We then realized that Bell, my sister wasn't with us. We searched all over the beach, but we couldn't find her. Then we went to the hotel and saw her playing games on the bed in the room.

The next day we all woke up and ate, brushed our teeth, took a bath and went to an amusement park a few miles away. We drove for 30 minutes and finally arrived there where we saw a lot of rides and games. We said "wow" as we looked around and then we went on a few of the rides and played a few games. After we got something to eat and then went home. The next few days were normal but on the fifteenth day we saw an octopus on the beach crawling around, we all grabbed our phones and took pictures. The octopus was brown and super cute. We knew that some octopuses are poisonous so we didn't touch them. On the twentieth, we went to a zoo and saw a lot of different animals. I even got to hold a snake and an alligator. On the twenty-fifth Bell caught a cold so she could not come out to the beach. Then on the thirtieth, she got better, and we all went to K.F.C. And ate then we went back to the beach. We also went on a boat and learnt how to catch fish. On the way to the sea, we saw whales, dolphins and a shark. All the other days were normal and then the holiday ended,

and I went back to school and told John everything that happened. Then told me that he went to the moon, then Mars, then Venus, but I didn't believe him, so he called his mom to confirm. She said that John was only dreaming and so I started laughing.

A Garden

by
Antwan Russell

A garden is a thing of beauty and a job forever. A garden is rectangular with a lot of fruits and vegetables. These fruits and vegetables need space as well as sunlight and water. Yesterday I looked at my garden and it was full of fruits and vegetables. Some are rotting but some are also beautiful. If you were to look inside my gardens you would see fruits and vegetables such as carrots, tomatoes, onions, mangoes, grapes and apples. My father watered my fruits and vegetables every day and I was able to build a trench around it so that the water could drain away.

When it's night time the plants are going to sleep or at least that's what I think they are going to do. "We can play now", said Mr Carrot. "It is time to start the party, let's play games and enjoy ourselves", stated Mrs Cabbage. All of the fruits and vegetables started dancing and then they jumped on the veggie-toy wagon and went to the veggie arena. In the back, sister Mango was playing music. She played while the other vegetables danced and enjoyed themselves. They drank their favourite beverage which was water mixed with fertilizer. The party continued while sister Mango played the music. Suddenly, the music stopped and Mr Broccoli walked in with Ms Celery and Aunty Parsley and all the other fruits and vegetables crowded them because they are big stars and are well known in the vegetable community. Everybody bought more water and continued dancing.

The garden doors busted open, and a large figure appeared in the smoke and began to grab all the vegetables. Some of them tried to escape but the figure caught up to them. Mr Broccoli, Aunt

Parsley and Mrs Celery tried to run but they all fell and got stomped to death. The ones who survived were thrown in the

back of a large van that was bigger than the veggie tray wagon. They all fell asleep and were awoken by the sound of other vegetables screaming for help.

The Plan: Evil In a Mother's Eye

by
Shalmell Morgan

A fresh dash of wind swept through the morning and weaved its way through the Mahogany trees in the backyard. The sun peeps through the cracks of the tree leaves and finds its way to bang on Pam's room window. The morning gave such delight and beauty when Pam Woke up. Her father was already at work while her mother was downstairs making breakfast in The kitchen. She went downstairs sleepily and then her mother asked if she was still going to Suzie's house. Then she remembered it was Saturday. Pam ran upstairs, packed her clothes and Snacks, had her bath, got dressed in her favourite clothes and dashed through the door before her Mother could even say goodbye.

At Suzie's house, Pam had a lot of fun. They played games and swam in Suzie's pool. At lunchtime, Pam called her mother many times without success. Suzie realized that something was wrong with Pm. She asked her "are you okay?" in a worrying tone. Pam replied, "yes I am o- o-okay". But she kept on asking until Pm told her she kept calling her mother but she did not respond. Suzie sighed and said "Pam go home, everything will be alright" The girls hugged each other and departed. When Pam went home, she saw her mother lying on the ground and her father standing over her with a bloody knife in his hand. She then realized that her father had stabbed her mother in her hand. Pam railed in the air and pushed her father away from her mother. Pam screamed in a nervous tone "run mommy run!" Pam's mother grabbed the knife, bolted through the door and jumped over the fence in their backyard.

Pam then started looking for her mother but could not find her. She then remembered that her mother had a friend living

a few blocks away named Kenjeon Briscoe. Pam hurried over to Kenjeon's house in search of her mother. When she got there and inquired about her mother, Kenjeon said her mother was not in the house. Pam stood at Kenjeon's door with a worried look on her face, contemplating where to go next. As she was about to walk off she heard a little voice in Kenjeon's house "she gone? Pam gone?" the voice inquired. Pam recognized the voice, pushed Kenjeon out of the way and went through the hall door. Only to see her mother with a nurse banding her hand. The bandage had spots of blood seeping through it.

Pam stood with eyes wide open and looked at her mother and asked "are you okay? ma'am? Her mother replied in an unbothered tone "Yes, yes I am good." Pam proceeded to ask her mother a lot of questions. Pam asked her "What happened to you and daddy?" her mother tried to explain- "your father thinks I'm cheating on him with Kenjeon so he did not go to work and spied on me". Pam held his forehead, spun around and questioned, "what nonsense is the lord?" Luckily Kenjeon bought plane tickets for us said Pam's mother. We have to leave early tomorrow morning, she said in a worried tone.

The next morning at about 7 o'clock they ate, took a taxi and went to the airport where they boarded their flight. Two days after living fearlessly in the United States of America (USA), Kenjeon sent a voice note to Pam's mother saying that Pam's father was arrested and he is the head of the lodge team. The lodge team needs a large amount of blood and her father has no family members so he goes around marrying people and killing them and their children. The reason for this is that he wants to be the richest man in the world. Pam rose in anger and disbelief, her mother hugged her and tried to keep her calm. Kenjeon called a few minutes later.

to ask if everything was okay. They told him yes and he advised them to stay in America for a few more days.

After a few days had passed Pam and her mother came back home. Pam's mother started to date Kenjeon and after five months they got married and began their lives together. Pam even got to see Kenjeon's twin boys Jamar and Shemar. The boys were very kind to Pam and her mother. Pam started attending school with the twins and two years later she graduated top of her class in all her subjects. Pam later applied and was accepted into the police force. There she met a kind man named Dashani Edwards. After speaking with each other time and time again they eventually became friends. They then started dating after three months and even months and later got married.

One day Pam told her husband that she was pregnant. He was over the moon, he lifted her and started shouting "congratulations to us!" They told their family member who congratulated them and nine months later Pam gave birth to twins, a girl and a boy. The boy was named Denile, and the girl Genile and the couple lived their lives and enjoyed their little family. However, their happiness did not last long. Two years later, Pam's father was released from prison. Pam and her mother began to get death threats from him. The father sent a text that allowed Pam to file a report at the police station. The text read "when I find out where you live I will kill everyone in your family including the twins." Pam was shocked and worried at the same time. The police tried tracking Pam's father with no success. The police reported that they didn't find anything suggesting that he left the country. Pam placed her father's picture on wanted signs around the community but still, nobody saw him. She afterwards added rewards and still, nobody reported that they saw him. The death threats stopped coming and Pam gave up and stopped looking for him. One day,while Pam was at work she saw her motherwith her father in a car. She told her coworker to stop the car and check its documents. Pam became even more worried than before. She called her superintendent to say she was not well and needed to go home as quickly as possible. While driving home, Pam saw an old man stopping and asking for a ride to go and get some vegetables at the market. She obliged and allowed the man to come in the car. Two minutes into the drive the man took off the disguise. Pam was shocked it was her father.

She let the steering wheel loose and started screaming. The car started to dilly-dally across the street. Her father quickly reached over and held the steering wheel. He managed to calm Pam down and proceeded to talk. Pam listened as he explained that he was her father, but he did not cut her mother as she thought. He explained that it was his twin brother. Pam's father said that their parents had some financial issues, so they gave his next brother up for adoption. Pam's father said that it was his twin brother that cut her mother and that her mother knew he had a twin brother and staged the entire thing. Pam did not believe what this man was saying but luckily the man had some proof of what he was saying. With this proof, Pam called her Backup officers to chase a red Nissan car which had a license plate reading 5368 MP. It turned out the man was telling the truth. Kenjeon and Pam's family members could not believe what was being revealed to them about the situation. Pam's real father's twin brother and her mother were taken to jail.

My First Day At School

by
Martina Miles

It was 6:30 am when I woke up to the sound of the alarm clock. My mom was yelling, "Martina! Martina! Get up! Or you will be late for school." Today is my first day at the Ranchman Primary school and I'm so excited to make some new friends. I hurriedly went to the bathroom, got dressed and then rushed downstairs for my breakfast. I had to eat my breakfast quickly because mom and dad were waiting for me in the car. After eating I went to the car and it was now time to leave for school. The drive was about ten minutes from my home to school.

When I got there the school compound was filled with boys and girls and I was so excited to see everyone happy. Because I was a new student I had to go to the principal's office first. While in the office I was introduced to my classroom teacher, Ms Foster. She took me to the classroom where I was introduced to my classmates. I felt welcomed in the class because my classmates were very friendly to me. It was now 10:30 am and the bell rang for a short fifteen-minute break. My classmates and I went to the tuck shop to buy our snacks. After the break period was over we went back to our classroom. Our teacher Ms Foster asked us to introduce ourselves and I was extremely happy to do so. This exercise took about ten minutes to be completed and then it was time for the hard work to begin.

Our teacher gave us a test to see what we had learnt from our previous school. The test lasted for half an hour, which then took us up to our lunchtime. Everyone was shouting because it was now lunchtime. The teacher told us to stand and say our graceand then we formed a line and went to the canteen to get our delicious lunches. After eating I went to the playground with my friends to play a game of "catch". We played for a while and then I went to get some water from the fountain before going back to class. After the lunch period, our teacher gave us another test to do, which was mathematics. It was my worst nightmare but I had to face it head-on.

When I completed the test I had a little break and I used it to speak to some of the other girls who also completed the test. Finally, I peeked up at the clock it said 2:30 pm and this meant that it was now time to go home. I cleared my desk, packed my bag, and stood up to say my evening prayer. After the prayer, I went outside to wait for my parents and when they got there I happily got into the car and told them what I experienced at school.

Contributions From Kindergarten

The Game

by
Nickayla Ball

Jack and Tom were playing football on the side of the road. They were having fun. Tom kicked the ball and slipped. The ball rolled in the street. Tom ran after the ball. A bus was coming and Tom was on the road. Tom picked up the ball; however, the bus almost hit him. A man held him and pulled him out of the street.

Play Day At The Park

by
Alexia Dryen

The day was bright and sunny; Jaden, Jermaine and Kenny went to the park to play a game of cricket. While the boys were playing, a bird flew into the tree above them. They all stop to look at the bird and notice that a nest was in the tree. Kenny was climbing the tree. The bird flew away. When Kenny held on to the limb it broke ad he fell to the ground. Jaden and Jermaine helped Kenny. His mom took him to the hospital. His hand was placed in a cast.

A Day At The Beach

by
Yendi Willie

47

The Williams family went to the beach. They looked happy. The day was bright and sunny. The sun was hot so the family went under a coconut tree to get some shade. Jackie and Tim went swimming. After that, they went to the beach to play a game of football.

Paths & Gateways Inc is an organization committed to helping children who reside in deep-rural communities in Jamaica to have fun learning and excel in various fields. We want to bridge the gaps that exist between them and other children who live in the more developed regions of Jamaica. We aim to promote Equity and Inclusion in the education, wellness, and psychosocial development of children.

www.pathsandgateways.org

Paths and Gateways